Journeying in Praise, Song and Worship

Journeying in Praise, Song and Worship

FLORA PARKER

CITI OF
BOOKS

CITIOFBOOKS, INC.

3736 Eubank NE Suite A1

Albuquerque, NM 87111-3579

www.citiofbooks.com

Hotline: 1 (877) 389-2759

Fax: 1 (505) 930-7244

Ordering Information:

Quantity sales. Special discounts are available on quantity purchases by corporations, associations, and others. For details, contact the publisher at the address above.

Printed in the United States of America.

ISBN-13:   Softcover   979-8-90124-002-1

                      eBook   979-8-90124-003-8

Enjoy this comforting short glimpse of a blessed long life embodied with faith ,work ,service ,and ultimately, reward.

— James Lofton-Hunter) grandson(

Mother Parker,

What a great accomplishment you have at hand !I have often heard you state" ,You don't know my story ",but with the completion of your memoir ,the world has been given a personal inside look .I am grateful to have you as my grandmother ,teacher ,and friend .May God continue to bless you richly!

Love,
Ja'Nay Lott

INTRODUCTION

At age eighty-four, I look back at life, and this seems like a good time to list some of the things I've lived through and learned from. In a quest for memories for my children, my grandchildren, my great-grandchildren, and the future generations, I thought it to be proper to make notes about life in days past and where I have grown to be.

This book is the start of pouring out thoughts and organizing them. It feels important to pass down history as I remember it, a time span that's not so long in the "big scheme," but one that encompasses vast changes in society, including the shift from farm life that so many lived just three generations ago. This change from living close to the land to living close to technology has dramatically shaped our lives and how we relate to one another and God. A look back into the recent past helps bring things into balance.

I also wanted to write about music as I've learned it and about living in the spirit of God, which I have always tried to do.

The indelible chord of music runs through my story just as it weaves through the fabric of American life, and music from sanctified and spiritual churches is still at the heart of almost every generation in our country. This is the beat of our lives, and this book is a look into a small portion of that history. I hope it advances our collective spirit.

1960-1963

The Road I Traveled

Tylertown is in the lush Mississippi countryside along Highway 48, about twenty miles southeast of McComb. In the mid-1930s, Tylertown had a Main Street and three other streets passing through it, but most residents lived on farms outside town. This is where I entered the world on August 6, 1936, the fifth of six children born to Willie Dillon and Linnie Travis Dillon.

I was born at home, with a midwife helping my mother, and she had an easy labor without complications. She was likely back to her chores and routine soon after my birth. We lived on a forty-acre farm where my father grew all kinds of vegetables, cotton, corn, and sugarcane. We had fruit and nut trees too, including peaches, pears, figs, plums, walnuts, and pecans. Harvest started sometime from mid to late July in the different fields and orchards and continued until early October.

My father also had an orchard of tung oil trees, which, although poisonous, were valued for the oil derived from the seeds of the berrylike fruit. The oil was traditionally used in lamps and, later, in paint, varnish, and motor fuel.

We also had cows, horses, chickens, ducks, geese, and hogs. We experienced, for the most part. four seasons: spring, summer, fall, and winter. The winter months were very cold, and sometimes we would get snow.

My father would make a big fire in the fireplace, and my mother, father, baby sister, and I sat around the wood fire eating pecans, peanuts, and walnuts. It would often rain throughout the year, and during hurricane sea-son, we would feel the storms. There were times we would be in the direct path of a passing storm and suffer great property loss. But God always took care of us. In the spring, the landscape would thicken with pines and oaks, berry bushes, and fruit trees. Mississippi is a beautiful state, one of the prettiest I have traveled through.

COUNTRY LIFE
DURING THE GREAT DEPRESSION

When I was young ,America was in the midst of the Great Depression and struggling to emerge from the Dust Bowl era ,but we lived a decent life .We were a blessed family .We always had food to ear because my father raised almost everything .The only things my parents had to buy from the store were staples such as flour ,tea .and coffee .We grew everything else ,and I remember tree collard greens reaching five feet tall ,tomatoes ,cabbage ,string beans, turnips ,black-eyed peas ,and green onions growing in rows as long as three truck beds.

Our land was a mix of fertile and poor soil. My father would add fertilizer to the poor soil and work it until it became productive. We were up at daylight, and I would help plough the fields, as I was the only one at home to help. Using a sweep plough, which is small, I would hook it up to the horse and step in unison with the horse. I was a fast stepper, and my dad said I did a good job. He labored with a mule and a heavier plough. We would have dinner at noon, rest for an hour, and then get the horse and mule and work until quitting time at four thirty. We ploughed year-round in phases. Late April and early May were busy, and the cotton would open in August, and we would start picking. My mother would help pick and hoe, and leave at 10:00 am to cook dinner. When Mama cooked, everybody loved it. She would prepare fresh vegetables from the garden and could create a meal using whatever was available. If she had only cornmeal, she would make delicious muffins. She would cook dumplings in chicken stock made from a previous meal, as well as treats like sweet potato pie, pound cake, and lemon meringue pie.

Additionally, Mother made our clothes and bedding, including quilts, bedspreads, and sheets. My entire family always dressed well. She used large flour sacks or remnants from the fabric stores. I learned to sew and began making my own clothes when I was about nine. My mother cooked on a woodstove. We finally got propane gas in 1948. My mother purchased a fifty-gallon propane gas tank and bought a black porcelain stove for our kitchen, and Mama began cooking with gas on the black beauty. We had to buy blocks of ice for the refrigerator until connected with electricity. Up until 1949 our source of lighting is a lamp that burn oil. I had to do my homework by lamp. It was hard to my eyes, yes, but I made it. When the electricity was connected in our area we then celebrated and thank god for the light. On the same year we got our first black-and-white TV. Telephone service arrived in 1951 with a five-party line.

Later my father installed propane gas heaters in all the three bedrooms, living room, kitchen, and dining area in the wood-frame house. The heaters provided welcome warmth to my bedroom. There was no bathroom in the house, and we had to go outside to use the bathroom. My sister Mary Elnora was the baby, and sometimes she would sleep in my bedroom and sometimes with Mama and Papa.

Sometime around 1947 or 1948, my father wanted to get a gas-burning refrigerator. A salesman came through our neighbor- hood offering gas refrigerators, and my father was sold on the idea. However, my mother did not think it would be that useful since we were already buying blocks of ice for our icebox and it would last for a week at a time. She did not think we needed the extra expense.

My dad made the decision to go ahead with the refrigerator, and my mother was very upset. This was the first and only time I heard my parents in a heated discussion. He felt it would provide a source for food and other things that required refrigeration, and she felt we needed to save for other expenses that might occur. My mother packed a few personal items on a plastic bag, I shall never forget she told my baby sister and I she would come back for us. When she walked out of the house with the plastic bag in her hands my baby sister and I started screaming, my dad was trying to make us quiet but nothing works. By this time my mom had made it on top of the hill down the road when my dad rush and catch up with her. I don't know what the conversation between them were, all I know is she won.

Well, she won. Dad contacted the salesman and had them come pick up the refrigerator, and life went on.

Sometimes our funds would be low, and my parents would raise Rhode Island chickens. They were beautiful. We had chicken pens for them, and when they reached a certain size, they could come out of the pen. The chickens would walk across the grass picking, but they would not go across the street. It was amazing how well they were trained to not leave our yard. Sometimes they would go to the edge of the road, but they did not cross the road. Before sundown, we would gather them up and they would march back to their pens in formation. When the chickens were fully grown, my parents would take one or two to town and sell them for somewhere between three and four dollars. At the time, that was big money, and we would put aside one dollar for gas, which was twenty-five cents per gallon. Our 1935 Chevy got good mileage, and we could go to town, church, and rehearsal.

FAMILY LIFE AND MUSIC

My father, Willie Dillon, was sharp and clean-shaven. He kept his hair cut short and groomed, and his two suits were immaculate. A religious man, he was a deacon in the church, and he was musically talented. After working in the fields all day, he would teach a cappella singing in the evening to church choirs. When I was around six years old, I began to go to choir practice with him because my mother and my baby sister, who was five years younger, could not go. He taught me to sing the three parts with the choir: soprano, alto, and tenor. When he was short a singer in any of the three parts, he would have me fill in. I loved to sing with the choir and would get a good, strong feeling, I felt like a big girl, and the choir members thought it was wonderful. We always sang gospel songs such as "What a Friend We Have in Jesus," "The Lord Will Make a Way Somehow," and one of my favorites, "Jesus, Keep Me Near the Cross."

Driving home from choir practice on the back county roads, I paid close attention to how my father shifted the gears and operated the vehicle. When I was ten, he would let me take the wheel and drive home. There were no paved roads. Even the main Highway 48 was gravel, but the public roads were well maintained. I was happy I could drive a car and got my first driver's license at age fifteen.

There were six of us siblings, and we had a wide age span between us, ranging from two years to six years apart. My baby sister and I were the only two who actually grew up together because my older siblings lived in dorms to attend school. Quincy Rudolph was the oldest, then Violene, Robert Toney, Oralean, myself, and Mary Elnora, the youngest.

We are a long-living family. Quincy passed away in 2016 and lived to age ninety-two. Violene was ninety-four and had moved back to Mississippi from Vallejo California where she had lived for forty years. She passed away in 2024. Robert is ninety-one and passed away 2021. Robert is ninety-one and lives in Sacramento and still drives himself to church. Mary is eighty and resides in Mississippi as well. However, Oralean Ryans had an untimely passing at age twenty-four. She was killed in an auto accident in Pinole, California, in January 1955. Four of us are yet alive to remember our shared history of Mississippi farm life.

As a child, I was interested in musical instruments, and we had a piano in our home. Quincy played the piano, the trombone, and the saxophone. We were the only two siblings who played music. I began sitting at the piano playing one key at a time to find the mel- ody I heard in my head. My parents started me with music lessons: however, I had no interest in learning to read music, although I could read the a cappella notes. I was highly interested in playing piano by ear. I played at every opportunity. I always played the music as I felt it and heard it in my mind. I felt joy as my fingers moved over the key- board, practicing in every key and continuing until I was satisfied. Music soothed me and still does to this day.

I remember my great-aunt on my father's side had a pump organ. I would try to play the organ, but my legs were too short to reach the pedals and I was not strong enough to make the sound come out. However, I had the desire to play the organ, and somehow knew I would play it later on. Music was part of our makeup.

I grew up with segregation, but I never had any problems because I always knew my place and stayed in my place. Our par ents taught us there were certain things we could not do, places we could not go, such as eating establishments, and certain doors we were not allowed to enter. There was a theater in town, but I never had the opportunity to go see a movie. We followed their guidance and hoped for a change. At that time, that was the only thing I knew. I attended a segregated school in Ginn Town, about twenty miles. from where we lived. My father had a school bus route and drove children to the school. At one time, he owned his own bus. Our community was predominately Black. Primarily due to segregation, our community was close-knit. There were times when my parents would leave to go church or into town and never have to worry about locking the doors.

Until I left, the Whites and Blacks did not mix well. Many of the Black families lived as sharecroppers because they could not afford to purchase land. My parents were blessed to purchase the forty acres of land where we lived. Ultimately, the land was divided among us siblings upon my father's death in 1994, as my mother passed away in 1984.

HEADING WEST

Early in life, I planned to finish high school, graduate, and go away for college. I focused on going north to Chicago where most of my friends were going, but I ended up moving to Vallejo, California, where Violene lived. I graduated from high school on a Friday night and left for California on Saturday morning in May 1953. My traveling companion was my five-year-old niece, Violene's old- est daughter, Betty Sue; and carrying one suitcase each, we boarded the Sunset Limited train out of New Orleans. We arrived in Los Angeles, changed trains, and headed north to Crockett, near Vallejo. I enrolled in Vallejo Junior College in the summer that same year.

While at Vallejo Jr. College, I met a young man named Timothy Douglas. He was recently discharged from the army, and he, too, was a student at the college. We would meet and talk in between classes. He was a Christian and a member of the Church of God in Christ. Pastor Garrett was the pastor, and the church had a large following of young people. I lived with Violene and attended the St. John Baptist Church in Vallejo.

Timothy and I were married at the Fifth Street Church of God in Christ on April 1, 1954. We moved to California's capital. Sacramento, and I enrolled in Sacramento City College. Timothy found a job. I finished out the year at City College and then enrolled in Thomas Real Estate School, where I obtained a real estate license. I worked for a while as an agent, but it was difficult because our first two children were fourteen months apart. Linda was born in 1954 and Virginia in 1955. The hours required in real estate were not suited for a family schedule. Timothy Jr. was born in 1957. All the while, we attended the Fifth Street Church of God in Christ. We moved to Galt, more out in the country, in 1964. We planned to have space for children from the church to have a place for recreation.

The church was located at Fifth Street and Capitol Avenue, Sacramento, California. Later, the church was moved to Broadway and Thirty-Seventh Street, its present location. Pastor Fegan changed the name of the church to Bethel Church of God in Christ. We had only a piano at the church, and there was a regular musician, Corrine Elby Fegan, who played, but she began to have trouble with her hands, and this affected her playing. So during one evening service in 1955, she walked to the pew where I was sitting and told me that I was playing for the service that night. I did not know what to say! I did not feel I could do it seeing as how I had never played for a service in the Church of God in Christ, and usually the songs are pretty upbeat.

Well, by the grace of God, I did it.

That was the beginning of my playing for the Church of God in Christ. It was some six or seven years later that the pastor, Elder Eugene Fegan, passed away. An interim pastor, Bishop Darrett, was there for a short period of time before appointing my husband, Timothy Douglas, as pastor. He acknowledged his calling, attended Sacramento Theological Seminary, became a minister, and served as pastor of Fegan Memorial Bethel Church of God in Christ for seventeen years.

I was playing the piano and asked if we could purchase an organ for the church. We purchased an organ for our home, and I taught myself how to play it using the same method I had as a child. by finding the melody I heard in my head. So he agreed on get- ting an organ for the church, and we searched around the different music stores and found a very, very good used Hammond Organ and purchased a Leslie speaker to go with it. Each organ has its own unique sound some have full foot pedals, some have half foot ped- als, and some have drawbars, while others do not. It's like purchas- ing an automobile. You can purchase one with many added features. For instance, adding a Leslie speaker gives depth to the sound. That Hammond B3 Organ and Leslie speaker are yet in that little church and yet have a great sound. moved to Galt, more out in the country, in 1964. We planned to have space for children from the church to have a place for recreation.

The church was located at Fifth Street and Capitol Avenue, Sacramento, California. Later, the church was moved to Broadway and Thirty-Seventh Street, its present location. Pastor Fegan changed the name of the church to Bethel Church of God in Christ. We had only a piano at the church, and there was a regular musician, Corrine Elby Fegan, who played, but she began to have trouble with her hands, and this affected her playing. So during one evening service in 1955, she walked to the pew where I was sitting and told me that I was playing for the service that night. I did not know what to say! I did not feel I could do it seeing as how I had never played for a service in the Church of God in Christ, and usually the songs are pretty upbeat.

Well, by the grace of God, I did it.

That was the beginning of my playing for the Church of God in Christ. It was some six or seven years later that the pastor, Elder Eugene Fegan, passed away. An interim pastor, Bishop Darre period of time before appoint Douglas, as pastor. He acknowl Sacramento Theological Sem

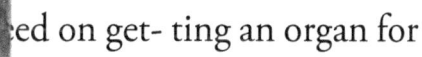

I ed on get-ting an organ for the church, and we searched around the different music stores and found a very, very good used Hammond Organ and purchased a Leslie speaker to go with it. Each organ has its own unique sound some have full foot pedals, some

have half foot ped- als, and some have drawbars, while others do not. It's like purchas- ing an automobile. You can purchase one with many added features. For instance, adding a Leslie speaker gives depth to the sound. That Hammond B3 Organ and Leslie speaker are yet in that little church and yet have a great sound.

1960-2019

I was married to Timothy Douglas for thirty-two years. During this time, 1 began working for the state of California. In mid-1960, I started as a temporary worker at the Franchise Tax Board at Tenth and N. Streets, Sacramento, California. After two months with the tax board, I interviewed for a position as a typist clerk with the DMV at Twenty-Fourth and Broadway, Sacramento, California, on the night shift from 5:00 p.m. to 1:00 a.m. This was a good shift because we did not have to get a babysitter. I worked some five years for the state before I became an entry-level eligibility worker with Sacramento County. After six months, I became an eligibility worker Il and continued with promotions. I was often in charge as a lead worker or filled in for a supervisor when needed. I retired from the county after twenty-four years. Upon retirement in 1991, I continued to work for Sacramento County as an on-call worker until 2012.

During this time, I wanted to have a business of my own and conducted a lot of research to open a self-serve Laundromat. I found a suitable building and priced commercial-grade washers and dryers. In 1980, I went to Bank of America and talked to a banker about financing for the Laundromat. Some of my relatives were skeptical that I would get a business loan. But I did, and we opened Douglas Sudz House. Three years later I opened a ladies' boutique the name of the boutique is Flora's Fashion and Alteration. Another year passed and I purchased a dry cleaner and finally, I ran a group home for troubled teenagers. For the group home, I was blessed to have very good pro- fessional help, including a director, a psychologist, and experienced care workers. Oftentimes the teenagers would flourish with extra care and attention. Later some of them would join me at church.

One morning in 1986. Timothy got up to go open the Laundromat, and he never returned. For me, it was like a bad dream. I never know why Timothy left home the way he did. He separated himself from me and his children. He would periodically contact the children. My oldest daughter told me that her dad told her he wanted to return home but he was afraid I would not accept him back. To my knowledge none of the congregation knew why he left the way he did.

I was very strong in the church, and my faith in God sustained me. I started attending a church in Chico, California, and for the next six years, I traveled to Chico every Sunday. I kept busy with work and travel.

A New Beginning

I met Rev. Aubrey Parker in March 1990. He was the pastor of the Philadelphia Missionary Baptist Church at 4020 Y. Street in Sacramento's Oak Park neighborhood. He heeded the call to ministry in 1978 and had a vision to organize a church in 1986.

The Philadelphia Church was organized in a Sacramento living room on May 12 at Rancho Lobo Court. Dr. John Blouin was the moderator. Six people were fellowshipped in as members. Rev. Parker delivered his first message as a pastor, "God Is Speaking Today," and read from Psalm 33:9, "For he speaak, and it was done; he commanded, and it stood fast." The first offering totaled $11.62. Services were held at the Rancho Lobo address for approximately three months.

Meanwhile, Rev. Parker found a former grocery store and then print shop on Y. Street and remodeled it to serve as the church. He named it Philadelphia, the church of brotherly love. His inspiration for the name was the book of Revelation 3:7. Philadelphia stood at 4020 Y. Street for thirty-three years.

In the beginning, there were Sundays when no one would show up. Rev. Parker would hold service anyway, immaculately dressed, singing, reading scriptures, giving testimony, and praying at the altar. He would check his watch, and when service was over, he would close up and head home. If anyone asked him how church was, he said it was just fine.

Church members introduced us to each other, but it took several tries for us to get together at a dinner party. I forgot to attend the first party, and he forgot the second. The third time was a charm, and we liked each other, although I was too busy to think much about it. However, he asked if he could keep some cows on my property in Galt, California, and I consented. Thus, he was able to return to care for the animals. We married on September 1, 1990.

I left the Church of God in Christ to serve with my husband in the Baptist ministry, which was not a hard thing to do because I had served in the Baptist denomination before. In July 1995, we attended a fourth Monday Union meeting in Stockton, California, with the Church of God in Christ, and he made the decision to fellowship and merge the Baptist Church with the Church of God in Christ. The church became the Philadelphia Church of God in Christ, but we stayed in our same spot on the corner of Y. Street and San Jose Way. The church door faced northeast, and we welcomed all who passed through.

Philadelphia had only a piano when I became a member, but no musician. So Rev. Parker decided after the merger that we would invest in an organ for the church. We went to music stores and found a used B3 Hammond Organ and a Leslie speaker. We both attended the Sacramento Theological Seminary and Bible College, where he earned a doctoral degree. I received a master's

Rev. Parker earned many awards, certificates, honors, as well as promotions. He was appointed as Emmanuel district superintendent, overseeing four churches and served fourteen years working to resolve issues and relieve burdens while always holding his peace. He was recognized and established as an emeritus district superintendent in 2016.

I served twenty-seven years as an Emmanuel district missionary with eleven appointments, including former president of area pastors' and ministers' wives, assistant supervisor of women, Sunday school superintendent, and choir organizer.

Rev. Parker and I lived happily together, and we were blessed to visit Jerusalem, the Holy Land, China, Europe, and the Caribbean. We also purchased a vacation home in Magnolia, Mississippi, which is about eighteen miles west of Tylertown, and furnished it as I saw it in my dreams. The home was built in 1894 and had a steeple, semiround front porch and four fireplaces. We visited there three or four times a year.

Celebrating in New home Rev. Parker Purchased for me. as a Wedding Gift To me.

We served together at Philadelphia Church for twenty-eight years and rejoiced in so many beautiful services, church anniversaries, and fellowships with God's family. We had teas, holiday musicals, and revivals; oftentimes, the spirit was so high the small church seemed to be bursting at the seams with holy praise. The Philadelphia church was a sanctuary where prayer and the gospel were always present, and we truly rejoiced in the day at hand. I continued to play the organ and felt like I hit my stride musically during this time. I was able to play and sing as I felt moved and channeled my praise and joy and tribulations into the music. One of our favorite songs in Philadelphia was "JESUS IS ON THE MAIN LINE, TELL HIM WHAT YOU WANT, CALL HIM UP AND TELL HIM WHAT YOU WANT."

I continued to support the church even when I was stricken with cancer in 2007. I missed one Sunday from church after surgery. The cancer returned in 2012, at which time I had to undergo a major surgery, which required me to take time off from my job. I returned to work three weeks later and worked for a short period of time, and then resigned from Sacramento County, but continued to operate my businesses while going through treatments. My youngest daughter, Virginia, was diagnosed with Lung Cancer and tragically passed away at age fifty-one. I didn't understand why God would take her at fifty-one and leave me at seventy-one. I could only think that my work here is not yet finished.

MANAGING THE MOMENT

Rev. Parker was such a strong man during our time together. You never really knew when he wasn't feeling his best. He was playful and had a great sense of humor. As the years advanced, his health became frail, and his memory did not serve him as well as in earlier days. Still, he was almost always in church, and we were fortunate to never be in poor health at the same time. I led many services, delivering messages with the pastor's blessing.

His health was diminishing when we went to Honolulu to celebrate our twenty-seventh anniversary. This was our last anniversary together. We were on the twenty-ninth floor of a beautiful hotel, with a room overlooking the ocean and a clear view of the sunset from our lanai. Dad Parker said he didn't feel like going out to eat and asked if I wouldn't mind going to get some take-out food. So I went out for food and came back to our room, but when

I walked into the room, he had a strange and confused look on his face. I said, "Babe, I got something I think you're going to really like." He said he did not know who I was. At first, I thought he was just kidding around, but he actually did not know me. I felt pain deep down inside my body. All I could do was to wrap my arms around him and hold him as tightly as I could. We were scheduled to leave in a couple of days. I called his doctor and explained to him what happened. The doc asked if he was in any pain. I told Dr. Fisher that he was not complaining of any pain. He advised me not to leave him alone and, should he become radical, to get him to the ER in Hawaii. He wanted to see him in his office as soon as we returned home. Rev. Parker came out of his confusion a little bit, and we stayed on the last few days in Honolulu, but he never left the room. He was never quite the same after that September in Hawaii.

The last several months of his life were long and empty because he did not have the drive I had always seen in him. Still, Rev. Parker was present at Philadelphia Church, and in November 2017, he presented a Bible to our great-granddaughter GennaLe Lott after her baptism. He led Philadelphia for thirty-two years before peacefully passing from this life on January 3, 2018, at age ninety-four. I still miss him. Our life together represented God's love and blessings.

MOVING FORWARD

After my husband's passing, I prayed mightily for Philadelphia Church to move forward in the absence of Rev. Parker. The Lord blessed the church, and souls were added. The modest but growing congregation brought fresh energy and vibrant activity to the church. Several of my children, grandchildren, and great-grandchildren attended Philadelphia and participated by singing, giving testimony, reading scripture, or ushering for special services such as Easter Sunday.

Philadelphia stood strong on the corner of Y Street until April 28, 2019, when we held our last service after an inspector from the city of Sacramento said we did not have the proper permit to operate a church. We were unsuccessful in convincing the city to "grandfather" in the church based on its long-term status in the neighborhood. Philadelphia enjoyed support from the surrounding neighborhood, but the $12,000 "conditional use permit" fee required by the city was prohibitive. Additionally, the fee would not be returned if the city denied the permit.

We moved out of the church on Monday, April 29, 2019, and I stood in the sanctuary one last time and recalled all of God's blessings upon Philadelphia and its congregation.

The owner sold the property, and the church building was demolished on July 13, 2019.

With the demise of Philadelphia, I returned to Bethel Church of God in Christ on Broadway to fellowship with Supt. William Hunt J. and First Lady Gloria Hunt, jurisdictional supervisor of women. I also continue to visit other churches and was recently asked to read scripture at St. Paul Missionary Baptist Church on Fourteenth Avenue. It's a large church with more than one hundred people in attendance, and I read without a microphone. Everyone heard me. I am grateful for a strong voice and give praise for a bountiful life.

My early years gave me confidence that I could accomplish things, and I had the ambition to open businesses and operate them successfully. I never thought of anything as a failure, but thought of everything as a stepping-stone to greater success.

As I look back, I really don't know how I managed all this while raising a family, but by the grace of God. I kept everything going with the help of my loving husbands, Elder Timothy Douglas Sr., and Supt. Aubrey Parker. I never put church on the back burner because I know God is the source of my strength. If asked about the secret of life, I would say, "Being able to recognize there is a supreme being, being open-minded and sensitive to the world in which we live, and recognizing and supporting the needs of others."

I am a representative of God and lead a Bible study at Bethel on Thursday evenings, continuing my ministry. The Hammond B3 Organ remains there, and I still play. The music flows as it has throughout my life, offering praise and glory to God for sustaining me through times both difficult and joyous.

Driver Flora

When Jurisdictional Supervisor of Women, Mother E. M. Devers, resigned, Mother Richardine Lucille Hunt was appointed Jurisdictional Supervisor of Women Department of the Jurisdiction. A Jurisdiction consists of several churches in different areas and cities in the state. A Bishop, who is elected, serves as overseer of the Jurisdiction, and the Bishop appoints the Jurisdictional Supervisor.

Supervisor Hunt chose me to be her driver, and I drove for her for some 12 years, and she also appointed me to the position of Financial Secretary of the women's department. I served in that capacity for 4 years as I continued to be her driver, and ultimately, she appointed me to the position of "Third Assistant" to her. Of course, this was indeed humbling for me to be thought of so highly and counted worthy to be trusted with these assignments.

Her area was rather large, from Redding, California, north, to Bakersfield, California, to the south, Sacramento and San Francisco, as well as the Peninsula areas. I drove all these places while yet managing to carry on the work I was assigned to in my local church. home and community. I am grateful to have had a supporting husband who was not selfish and allowed me the privilege to serve.

Forever in my heart

In loving memory

IT JUST MAKES SENSE.

On this day, July 29, 2024—87 years, 11 months, and 29 days into my life's journey—I set my mind to leave on record the new chapter of my life, inspired once again by the Lord to write.

I look back with gratitude on the past and forward with great hope for the future. My greatest desire is to live forever with my Maker, my Lord and Savior, Jesus Christ. When I picture the place He has prepared for me, I see it like the setting sun in the evening sky. A blazing ball of fire sinks into the far west, so bright and near it seems as though one could drive toward it and catch it before it disappears. Watching the sun slowly hide itself behind the horizon is both majestic and electrifying—a glimpse of eternity in creation.

In recent months, I have often found myself lying awake in bed, unable to fall asleep. My mind is full: of family, of friends, of life itself. Yet I remind myself—I am charting the course, pursuing the dream. I am a conqueror. Through challenges, my experiences have shaped me into one who overcomes.

I reflect often on the seasons when my husband and I would plan our travels. He would count down the days and weeks until the next trip. Yet it seemed that each time we made plans, something unexpected would happen to delay or cancel them. Still, across our 27 years of marriage, we were blessed to travel far and wide—journeys to Hong Kong, Jerusalem, and countless smaller trips across the United States.

My husband has now been gone for seven years. Yet even now, I feel his presence every morning I awake and live another day. At times, I almost hear his voice, for he was a loving, kind, and devoted man. People often ask me, "Why do you still visit him so often?" My answer is always the same: It just makes sense.

Even as I carry his memory, I continue to pursue my dreams and walk in my calling. I am often asked to minister to young women as well as senior women. At my local church, I organized a widows' ministry where I have been blessed to encourage widows and widowers alike. To see others lifted

OUR EXTENDED family

up, to share kind words, kind deeds, and love—it just makes sense.

Recently, I celebrated my 89th birthday. To my surprise and delight, I was showered with gifts from the widows' ministry group. Their thoughtfulness touched me deeply. My heart's prayer is that I may continue to be a blessing to others, especially to those less fortunate than I am.

Looking back, I know I have been truly blessed. My family and friends have supported me during times when loneliness and discouragement weighed heavily on me. And when I consider my life as a whole, I can truly say: I don't look like what I've been through.

I am a two-time cancer survivor. I have faced other serious health challenges, some of which required hospitalization. Yet I made it. By God's grace, here I am—still able to drive, able to care for myself, still able to live.

Through it all, I have learned this simple truth: life is not about avoiding hardship, but about trusting God through it, rising above it, and using your journey to help others. And when I look at my life, my calling, and my blessings—truly, it just makes sense.

Carrying Genna's Light :A Grandmother's Promise

This story is about my granddaughter, **JaNay Lott,** the mother of my great-granddaughter, Genna, who is now under my guardianship.

On **January 11, 2024,** our lives changed forever. JaNay had not been feeling well and decided to lie across her bed to rest. Hours turned into days. Her children, thinking she was simply exhausted, let her "sleep." After two days, her son finally called me and said words that shook my soul:

"Grandma, we can't wake Mom."

My heart froze. I asked what he meant, and when he told me she had been asleep for two days, I immediately rushed to her home, just eight miles away. I pulled into the driveway, ran into the house, and called her name. No response. I shook her gently, then more firmly—but her body was cold.

Across the street stood a fire station. In a panic, I ran, pounding on the door until someone answered. With all the breath I had, I pleaded, *"Please, I need help—something has happened to my granddaughter."* The firemen came quickly, but when the Fire Chief checked her, he turned to me with sorrow in his eyes and said, "She's gone."

I can still hear those words echoing in my heart.

I called my pastor, who came with the First Lady to comfort us. JaNay had been a faithful member of the church and led the Children's Ministry. The bereavement committee stepped in to help plan her service, but no committee, no words, and no rituals could fill the void she left.

———————————————————————————

JaNay was a **beautiful young mother of two**. After high school, she worked at Bank of America. She was always well-dressed, dignified, and respectful. A single mother, she carried her responsibilities with grace.

Her first child, **DeJay Marcel Lott**, was born with autism. Though it came with challenges, his life was precious, and she fought for his care and opportunities. Ten years later came her daughter, **Genna**, the little girl who would forever change my life.

When Genna was born, JaNay was working long hours, so I stepped in to care for her. My husband and I grew deeply attached to this child—our little angel—and she stayed in our home for 13 years. When JaNay passed, I became her legal guardian. Though the loss has scarred her, Genna has remained resilient.

Today, **Genna is 16 and a half years old**, in her junior year of high school, and dreams of attending college in Houston, Texas, to become a doctor. She has just completed her driver's training, and I could not be prouder. She still struggles with flashbacks of her mother's passing, but I see strength in her eyes every day.

JaNay's life was not without trials. At one point, she married a minister from our church, but the relationship brought her more sorrow than comfort. The marriage lasted only seven months. She carried the burden of betrayal, hidden grief from losing her parents, and the overwhelming responsibility of raising two children—one with special needs—largely on her own. She filed for divorce but passed before the proceedings were finalized.

Even in the midst of financial and emotional setbacks, the Lord has never failed us. He continues to meet our needs and carry us through.

Now, at 89 years old, I look at Genna and pray daily for strength and longevity. My greatest desire is to live long enough to see her walk across that stage at college graduation, stepping into the future her mother could not.

Though JaNay is gone, her light lives on in Genna. And as long as I have breath, I will carry that light forward.

LIVING TO LIVE AGAIN

When I first started working for the County of Sacramento, I never imagined where life would take me. I began as a clerk and spent five years in that role before moving on to become a case manager, helping people who had fallen on hard times and needed financial assistance just to survive. I understood them, because I, too, carried dreams—dreams of one day owning a Ladies' Boutique.

My plan was simple: work for a while, gain stability, then follow my heart. After I married Reverend Parker, I retired from the Sacramento County Department of Social Services and opened that boutique. But that wasn't my first step into business. While still working for the county, my husband and I opened a self-serve laundromat. It was a family operation. Our three children pitched in by mopping floors, cleaning spills, and keeping the place tidy. We gave them a salary, which taught them responsibility.

This was in the early 90s, when things were simpler—before the destruction and lawlessness we often see today. We even had an older gentleman neighbor who watched over the laundromat when we were away. Eventually, I sold the laundromat and focused on my boutique, conveniently located across the street in a strip mall. That shop was my pride. But soon, another calling tugged at me: becoming a foster parent.

My first placement was a set of 2 sisters. One resisted Sacramento, preferring her hometown, while the other embraced life with us. She was intelligent, respectful, and traveled with us even on out-of-state trips. I was proud when she graduated high school, though saddened when she had to move on.

The next placement was a 10-year-old girl who seemed wise beyond her years, shaped by a military family and life with her grandmother. Then came a 14-year-old from San Francisco, street-smart and hardened by her experiences. Alongside them was my granddaughter, who lived with us through her high school years. We gave her a car—a 1995 Mercury Cougar—so she could drive to school and work.

That car became the center of one of the most difficult foster parenting experiences I faced. One Saturday morning, I woke to find the Cougar missing. Moments later, the San Francisco Highway Patrol called. The two foster girls had taken the car, crashed through a toll gate, and wrecked it against a brick wall. By God's grace, no one was hurt. But the car was totaled, and I knew then that those two together were not a good fit for our home.

My final placement was perhaps the most meaningful: five siblings whose mother was battling addiction. She loved her children deeply but knew she couldn't care for them while under the power of drugs. She entered treatment, struggled at first, then realized the cost of failure would be losing her children forever. With time, she complied with the program, completed rehab, and reclaimed her life—and her family.

During their time with us, the children became part of our church family. When their mother was released, she joined us too, and later became a faithful member until her passing. Before she died, she made one last request— that I deliver her eulogy. Humbled, I honored her wish.

Her eldest daughter took responsibility for the younger ones, keeping them together in the home their mother had rented. It was not an easy path, but it was a loving one. I still keep in touch with that family, and each time I see how far they've come, I am reminded of why I opened my heart and home to foster children in the first place.

I have lived many lives—as a county worker, entrepreneur, boutique owner, foster parent, and minister's wife. Through each season, I have carried one truth: I am living to live again, when this life shall have passed.

It just makes sense.

OUR EXTENDED family

CHAPTER: WHEN FAITH MEETS THE FIRE

In the spring of 2007, I walked into my doctor's office for my yearly physical, expecting nothing out of the ordinary. I felt fine—no pain, no discomfort, nothing unusual. It was just routine.

A few days later, a card came in the mail requesting that I return for another mammogram. When I called, I was told they had seen a small spot. They wanted to take another look to make sure it wasn't something serious.

After the second mammogram and X-rays, the results were still inconclusive. The doctors ordered a biopsy. That's when the truth came to light: I had breast cancer in my left breast.

The doctor explained I should have the tiny mass removed immediately to prevent it from spreading. It was overwhelming—so much, so fast. My husband and I sat down to pray and talk. In the end, his words settled it for me: *"It's for your good. It just makes sense."*

At that very same time, my second daughter, Virginia, was also undergoing treatment for what doctors first thought was a respiratory illness. But when her condition worsened, further testing revealed Stage 4 lung cancer.

Our diagnoses came at nearly the same time. Mother and daughter, both stricken with cancer. I couldn't help her, and she couldn't help me. My heart ached.

Virginia was my jewel. She never forgot me, always doing something special for holidays or birthdays. Once, she surprised me with a trip to Germany. Whenever I needed help with church projects, I could count on her—and she'd bring her friends too.

She was bright and ambitious. After high school, she married a military man and traveled overseas. Though that marriage didn't last, she raised three children and pursued her dream of becoming a lawyer. She enrolled at the University of Northern California, Lorenzo Patiño

School of Law. She was scheduled to march with her class on May 11, 2008.

But God had other plans. Virginia passed away before that day. Her daughter marched in her place and accepted her Jurisprudence degree, tears streaming, love carrying her forward. Through it all, her older sister—who remained healthy—stood faithfully by her side, offering strength, comfort, and support for both Virginia and for me. That bond between the two sisters reminded me that even in the valley of illness and loss, love still held us together.

I was left asking questions that pierced my soul: *Why take my 51-year-old child and leave me, 71 years old?* God did not owe me an answer. His ways are His own.

So I chose to keep moving. I returned to work in my church and community. I even ran for a seat on the Oak Park Community Services Advisory Board and won, serving four two-year terms. I later became president of the Juvenile First-Time Offenders Board.

But in 2012, cancer struck again. This time, it returned to the same breast, stronger and more aggressive. My doctor recommended a mastectomy. After prayer and consultation, I chose a bilateral mastectomy.

The road ahead was not easy, but it was not unbearable. My recovery was smooth, the pain manageable. I missed only two Sundays at church. Though chemotherapy and radiation cost me my hair, they could not touch my spirit. Today, I am grateful to say: I am cancer free. To God be the glory.

Yet cancer still tried to creep into my life through my family. My youngest son, my baby, was diagnosed with blood cancer. His fight is ongoing.

Through it all, one truth has held me steady: what I have faced has not been failure, but stepping stones. Every trial, every test has refined me, not broken me.

When faith meets the fire, only God's purpose remains. And in the end—It just makes sense.

I lost my hair
from Treatment
of chemo and
Radiation

CONTINUING IN MY JOURNEY, MY JOURNEY CEASES NOT TO END

I sat down one morning, had made a cup of tea and around 9 AM, my phone rang. I answered, it was my eldest grandson calling. It took me a minute to recognize the caller because he seldom calls me, and I did not recognize the telephone number.

His voice did not sound as usual as he said "Grandma somebody needs to check on Uncle Junebug." I said, 'What do you mean? What's wrong?" He said, "He has trouble walking, and his apartment is very dirty." I was sitting down and had thoughts of where I could go and shop for new things, I was telling myself to get something different. I have nice clothes, but a lot of them are dated, yet are in good shape to wear. I get a lot of comments. I love clothes, so the messenger gave the message that my son was in dire need. So I laid everything down, dismissed the thought of clothes from the new and different clothing and the trip I was planning to take when my granddaughter would get a break from school or end the semester.

We did go on a five day trip in November 2024, this trip was also coupled with a business matter. So I went to my son's apartment, and the first thing I did was picking and cleaning trash. My son assured me that he was alright. "I asked how can you be alright when you are lying in bed?" So he kept saying he would be alright. I asked if he had been to a doctor, and he responded "No." He was taking some kind of over the counter pain pills, and some vitamins. I did not bother to see what kind of vitamins he had. I began to pray silently, asking God to give me what, and how, to work with the situation at hand. I called my daughter Linda, and talked to her about the situation, and told her I had to do something to get him to a doctor. He is a veteran, and can go to the veterans hospital and clinics that offer all services, including transportation. He refused every offer I presented to him to go see a doctor.

So I sat with Linda, and we talked and shared ideas. Finally, the Lord gave me to borrow my sister in law's son's wheelchair. When I made the call to my sister in law, Pearl Dillon, she said, 'Of course you can use it." On Monday, Linda went over and got the chair, and picked me up as we went to the apartment. I rode the wheelchair in, and my son asked, "What's all this about?" I told him I was taking him to the doctor, to have an assessment done, and to get an answer why he is barely walking, and has severe pain when weight is put on his hip bone area. I told him I got the wheelchair, because I said it would be difficult for him to go down the stairs and walk the distance to leave the building.

It took us about 45 minutes to get him into the wheelchair, and once we got out of the building, we put him in the car. Linda was the driver, and we took him to Mather Airforce Base Hospital. We sent my great granddaughter Genna, into the hospital to grab a nurse or whoever was available, to help him get out of the car. A nurse came running out with a hospital wheelchair, loaded him on, and took him inside.

They immediately said they would need to admit him, and began to test him and start giving him blood transfusions. The initial intake of blood was 5 pints. He stayed in the hospital for 8 days. Currently he has to go twice a week to be checked for his blood count, and has had several transfusions. He was diagnosed with Melanoma Cancer, and he has lesions over his entire body. I contacted the social worker to see if my son could have medical transportation. The social worker checked his eligibility, and he qualifies for transportation from his apartment and to be returned.

I tried to find out what the problem was where we could not get it set up right away. The social worker checked and was able to get it resolved, so he is eligible for transportation to and from for his treatments. It seems my lot to carry the burden, no matter what comes or goes, I will continue to do whatever I can do as long as I am physically able. Come what may, I will continue the journey. I am blessed on the journey. One day the journey will end.

I got up one Monday morning to make my granddaughter some breakfast and drive her to the light rail for her trip to school. After leaving her off at the light rail station, I returned home and began to feel a heaviness in my chest, so I called my doctor to see if I could get an appointment, but she was fully booked. I spoke to the advice nurse, and she began to explain what was going on. She put me on hold and came back on the line saying, 'I am calling an ambulance to pick you up and bring you to the hospital." These words were shocking to me. She said, "You need to be at the hospital." Within seconds the paramedics were here.

They began to check my vitals and within minutes, they were ready to take me to the hospital. I told them I didn't have a key to the house, and they asked, 'Well how do you get in?" And I said, "Through the garage with the garage door opener." They replied asking where the garage door opener was, and I simply replied, "In the car." So, they went to the car and got the garage door opener, and said, "We can leave now for the hospital."

They drove me to Mercy Hospital, and they took me to the emergency department. The emergency room doctor came over and began to examine me, and said, "We are going to have to admit you." I replied asking why, and he said, "because have you ever heard of congestive heart failure?" And I replied, "I heard the name before." The doctor told me I could have a heart attack in minutes. So I was admitted, and they immediately began to test me, but Thank God they found nothing very serious.

The Lord has been favorable unto me, and I will serve him the rest of my days. My greatest hope is looking beyond where I am now, and until then.

ABOUT THE AUTHOR

F lora Parker is a licensed evangelist missionary who serves in many capacities in her community and church. She is a speaker, organizer of youth and adult choirs, musician, coordinator of Widows Ministry, and vice president of Sacramento Valley Ministers' Wives.

Ministers' Widows (SVMWMW), Bible reader, business owner for some twenty years, an example for youths and young adults shaping their lives to be productive. She is a volunteer with the Surter Patient Family Advisory Team, productive in their quest for the future. Sutter Hospital in Sacramento, California.

She received a master's degree from the Sacramento Theological Bible College. She is retired from the Sacramento County Social Services Department. Sacramento, California.

She is active with her local church, Showers of Blessings Church of God in Christ. Dr. Darnell Thomas is her pastor She resides in Sacramento, California.